The Golden Age Of
BRITISH STEAM
Railways

COLIN GARRATT
on the work of
THE REV. AWH MACE

The Golden Age Of
BRITISH STEAM
Railways

From the Early Twenties to the Late Fifties

SUNBURST BOOKS

P.3 PHOTOGRAPH: An LNWR Tank Engine presumably on pilot duties in LMS days. Is the man on the gantry fixing the signals, or taking his own version of this photograph?

P. 4-5 PHOTOGRAPH: The G.W.R. Mixed Traffic Dean Goods, 0-6-0s once totalled 260 engines built between 1883 and 1899. Here one is seen heading a northbound goods near Culham.

Copyright © 1994 text & design Sunburst Books
Copyright © 1994 photographs Colin Garratt / Milepost

This edition first published 1994 by Sunburst Books,
an imprint of The Promotional Reprint Company Limited,
Deacon House, 65 Old Church Street, London SW3 5BS.

ISBN 1 85778 108 2
Printed and bound in Hong Kong

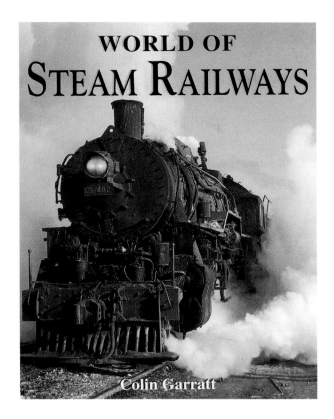

WORLD OF STEAM RAILWAYS

Colin Garratt

MILEPOST

This book has been produced in conjunction with Milepost 92½, which comprises
a team of talented individuals led by Colin Garratt, specialising in audio-visual production,
photographic services and a picture library for the Railway Industry.

For further information on Milepost 92½'s activities, please contact:

**Milepost 92½,
Newton Harcourt,
Leicestershire,
LE8 9FH,
England.**

Tel: (44) 0533 592068

BRITAIN'S RAILWAY
THE ONLY TRANSPORT FOR THE FUTURE

COLIN GARRATT

INTRODUCTION

This book introduces an important name to be included in the history of railway photography. The photographic legacy of the Rev. A.W.V. Mace will probably be the last major collection of steam age pictures to be discovered.

My introduction to Arthur Mace's widow Helen came through Michael Blakemore and Phil Atkins of the National Railway Museum. I made visits to Helen's delightful cottage in the Yorkshire Dales during the early summer of 1994 to discuss the prospect of Milepost publishing, cataloguing and conserving the collection. It was a time of great excitement as Helen herself was at that time preparing for ordination to the priesthood. For Helen, this book is a tribute to her late husband she had suggested to him several times the possibility of doing a book, but he showed little interest, replying that enough railway books were being published. However, he valued each photograph as he valued each day of his life, but underestimated their worth in collection. Until his last months teaching, ministry, and work in the Railway Museum and in his dark room kept him busy.

A.W.V. Mace was born in 1908 and died in 1986. He was brought up in Catford, South East London and educated at St. Dunstan's College. In 1936, he was ordained in Canterbury Cathedral, and throughout his scholastic career combined being a chaplain with teaching physics. He taught at St. Lawrence College Ramsgate and Rugby School before moving to Birmingham as a Gulbenkian Fellow in the Physics Department of Birmingham University. Subsequently he worked as a parish priest in the diocese of York for ten years.

It was Helen's wish that, in preparing the pictures for publication, Arthur's interpretation of the negatives be followed. This posed a problem. Firstly, the choice of pictures from thousands of negatives is my personal one had Arthur been here to choose them he might well have made a different selection. Secondly, cropping of photos is personal too. A conductor interprets the work of a great composer, and conductors renditions of a particular work vary, so it is impossible to say which is closest to the composer's ideal.

During the preparation of this book, I went through virtually every railway picture Arthur Mace made over a sixty-year period. I had never done anything like this before, and realised how very revealing photography is. Books are revealing in the same way - one gets very close to an author by studying what he has expressed. After examining thousands of Arthur's negatives, I felt I knew the man, although we never met. His impulses and vitality are as real to me now as if I had known him. And he liked people - this is so evident in his photography and of course in his teaching and ministry.

Over the years, Arthur Mace used many different sizes of negatives: 3¼" and 4¼" glass plates; 2½" x 4¼" on 116 or 118 Roll film; 6 x 9cm on 120; 6 x 6cm on 120 and 35mm.

I have been extremely fortunate in having the collaboration of Gerry Broughton, former head of photography at Southfields College, Leicester. Gerry who is a photographer, film historian and archivist, did the printing - painstakingly creating the very maximum each negative would yield. He felt an affinity with Arthur Mace too - in Gerry's own words: "He frames his pictures in a meticulous, almost whimsica,l way. The framing is often dictatorial and, if tampered with, the picture will fall to bits. His use of the environment and trackside features constitutes a theatre set with the train the actor, or sometimes merely filling a hole. Yet he was an opportunist he grabs a situation and some of the risks have paid off. Technical sacrifices are made for the sake of mood - he was never afraid to work in difficult conditions. He did the best he could, happy to leave the problems to posterity - in this case us".

His dentist corroborates this opportunistic trait. When he visited her surgery he normally brought two cameras with him " in case he saw something interesting on the way home".

One difficulty in selecting and cataloguing the pictures was the paucity of notes Arthur Mace made. Doubtless he knew every subject and remembered every picture but sadly his memories died with him, and the full story surrounding many pictures will never be known. In this respect I am indebted to R. C. Riley for his help in identifying many scenes and placing them into context through a keen eye and a lifetime's railway experience.

Arthur Mace was ahead of his time. His approach was completely natural, never stilted, and elements are included in his pictures that would at that time have been regarded as a nuisance. His spirituality led him to savour each moment and regard it with appreciation, making the social aspects of his work all-pervading. It is as if he were taking the pictures for posterity, faithfully recording scenes which were commonplace then, but in the knowledge that one day they would be fascinating. It is in these areas that his greatness lies, allied to the sheer diversity of his approach - an incredible variety of angles and distances, which again was unusual for his day when most railway photographers traditionally were three-quarter front view orientated. There is no doubt in my mind that he was one of the greatest railway photographers, amongst whose number I believe his name will rank with them after the publication of this book.

As the captions in this volume are of necessity short, perhaps it would be appropriate for me to make a few comments on eight chosen pictures.

Page 17 Lower. One of the most harrowing railway images of all time, and taken in extremely difficult light. The breaking up of this superb locomotive rendered an entire dynasty extinct. The Claughton stands in all its period magnificence complete with bag on chimney - the ultimate touch of pathos - against the austere setting of the cutting up shed at Crewe works.

Page 53 Upper. The finest picture of a London North Western Coal Engine I have ever seen - the engine's shape is beautifully accentuated in this definitive angle.

The chimneys, slate roofs, signal box and yard all personify 0-6-0 territory and augment the veteran at centre stage.

Page 62 Lower. Water-troughs were one of the most dramatic aspects of the steam age, and very under-photographed, particularly that moment when the fireman omitted to raise the scoop early enough, causing a geyser of water to shoot skyward, cascading over the leading coaches, entering through open windows and swirlinng down the corridors and entering the compartments.

Page 57 Lower. Another unforgettable picture of the decline of the London and North Western Railway dynasty, resulting from the Midland Railway's domination of the LMS's motive - power policy, and the rapid emergence of Stanier's designs during the 1930's. It is the summer of 1939 at Crewe works only months before the outbreak of World War Two. How many of the engines won a brief reprieve owing to the greatly increased need for locomotives for the war effort?

Page 24/25. This picture of the "Royal Scot" at Glasgow Central has a Picture Post feel which characterised much of Arthur Mace's work. It exudes an atmosphere of Britain in better times when our national pride, morale and social structure was intact - when we were looking forward with hope, yet proud of our past - and there was the sheer joy of steam trains which added so much to the quality of our lives.

Page 32 Lower. Arthur Mace had a great sense of humour and joy detectable in many of his pictures, but never more than here. The occasion was a Rugby School Railway Society outing to Leamington, presumably to see some "Bulldogs", "Stars" and "Saints" rather than the dreary London and North Western "Weaser" trundling through on the middle road.

Page 111 Upper. In contrast, this is one of Arthur Mace's opportunist shots. A stream-liner approaches at speed - clearly with little warning - and the two spotters, desperate to identify it, literally throw themselves at the fence. Did they succeed or was this fish the One that got away? The magic of trainspotting, the fleeting instant, the passion and thrill of the chase are all encapsulated in this amazing picture. And we today - fifty years later - still wonder which one that A4 was.

Arthur Mace's work comes from a golden age. It was as fabulous as we remember it to be, time has not added a rosy glow. Following the disappearance of steam in Britain, I spent twenty - five years professionally documenting on film the last steam locomotives of the world. The sights I saw - which included the extensive building of steam locomotives in China - are well documented elsewhere, but throughout I relived the golden days of my childhood with railways in Britain. Now we can all relive that amazing period of man's industrial progress through the pages of this book.

It is a mixture of pathos and ecstasy, for these pictures remind us of how much our railway has lost, to the detriment of society. The railway, once Britain's premier industry, has been decimated. The hideousness of our motorway network, the billions of pounds squandered on roads, with all their inefficiencies, point to one of the 20th century's most disastrous social policies. And those policies, which fly in the face of all logic, continue to be perpetrated today. If the railway is, as Churchill said. "the agent of civilisation", then the motor car is the agent of self - centredness, crime and life - threatening pollution. The road system of today has not evolved by being what is right for the nation, rather more it shows how vested interests can prevail - which tails can wag the dog.

Twenty thousand locomotives which served the nation's transport needs in a safe, disciplined and properly co-ordinated system have been replaced by millions of road vehicles which have settled on our society like a plague of flies.

The steam railway, as seen through the lens of Arthur Mace, teaches us much about transport today. It shows clearly that the railway did, and still could, provide a national transport system superior to anything we presently have - commercially, industrially, residentially and socially. No one with an ounce of social conscience could deny the truth of these words, particularly with road traffic expected to almost double over the next thirty years.

I, along with millions of others, want to see our railway serve society again as it did when the pictures in this book were taken. Sadly, it would not be with steam, for the world does move on, and change is inevitable. But callous planning based on vested self- interest is not so much change for the better as collective insanity.

I doubt whether Arthur Mace would have disagreed with these sentiments. He travelled avidly by rail to every corner of Britain in the days before fifty-percent of our railway network was wantonly shut down.

It is some small source of pride to me that this book was put together at Milepost alongside photography, audio visuals and videos for the present railway industry. We, as a railway production company, are doing all in our power to promote the just cause of the industry.

All who have worked on this book feel an over-riding sadness that Arthur Mace did not live to see it produced. I hope Arthur's dear widow Helen will enjoy the reflected glory this book brings, for she has made its publication possible. I hope she will be pleased by what we have produced.

Finally, it is my privilege to sign this introduction on Arthur Mace's behalf and in his memory.

Colin Garratt
August 1994

The subtle lines of the London and North Western Experiment 4-6-0s were tantalising. Introduced in 1905 as a 4-6-0 version of the Precursors with 6' 3" diameter wheels, their principal purpose was to work the more difficult northern section of the L.N.W. Main Line.

The majesty of the re-built Claughton is epitomised in this study of No. 5975 "Talisman".

A spectacular rendition of one of Webb's London & North Western 2-4-2Ts. Location unknown.

A Highland Railway Ben Class on freight duty.

A British Railways Standard Clan Class Pacific passes through Carstairs.

An exotic mix at Shrewsbury featuring a London & North Western rebuilt Claughton, a Great Western Pannier Tank and in the far distance a Cambrian Railway 0-6-0.

A London and North Western George V 4-4-0 approaches Chester.

This picture was taken on a party visit to Crewe Works during the 1930's when London and North Western Cauliflowers were still being given major overhauls. Behind is a Princess Royal Pacific and an L.M.S. Garratt.

A rare scene from Bow Works on the North London Railway with a London Tilbury & Southend 4-4-2T and L.M.S. Jinty 0-6-0T receiving overhauls.

Another view of the Erecting Shop at Bow Works featuring a North London 0-6-0T, an L.M.S. 3F 0-6-0 and a London Tilbury & Southend 4-4-2T.

A moment in history with the last London & North Western Precursor 4-4-0 No. 25297 "Sirocco" and the last Prince of Wales 4-6-0 No. 25752 awaiting breaking up at Crewe in 1949.

The last London & North Western Claughton No. 6004, outside the scrapping shed at Crewe Works in 1949. Originally "Princess Louise", this magnificent engine lost its name to the new "Princess Royal" No. 6204 in 1934.

The last of Fowler's 2-6-4T for the L.M.S.had side window cabs and this one - a Saltley engine - is seen with a local in the Birmingham area.

Fowler 2-6-4T No. 40043 was a Watford engine and is seen here with a Watford to St Albans train. A Bakerloo Line tube is in the background.

L.M.S. Fairburn 2-6-4T No.42684 at Shoeburyness. A Stanier three cylinder 2-6-4T built specially for the London Tilbury and Southend section can be seen on shed in the background.

No. 2500 was the first of Stanier's three cylinder 2-6-4Ts for the L.T.S. line. The first five of these engines were run in on Euston to Watford locals.

L.M.S. Jinty 0-6-0Ts were almost exclusively associated with shunting although they did work transfer freights.

London & North Western George V 4-4-0 No. 25245 "Antaeus" was a regular engine into Euston during the 1930s with outer suburban local trains with North Western stock.

L.M.S. Jubilee Class 45580 "Burma" bearing a Blackpool shedplate having been a Scottish engine for many years.

A B.R. Standard 9F 2-10-0 heads a southbound freight through Market Harborough. This scene has changed little over the forty years since this picture was made. Today, colour lights have replaced the semaphores and, of course, the cars are more modern.

The up Mid-day Scot enters Carlisle Station behind Princess Coronation Pacific 46250 "City of Lichfield" on the 2nd September 1952.

One of Fowler's original parallel boiler "Royal Scot" Class 4-6-0s as introduced in 1927 for the L.M.S.

The intensely exciting and all enveloping atmosphere of the engine sheds during the "Golden Age" had to be experienced to be believed. Here an L.M.S. Crab 2-6-0 and two Stanier 8F 2-8-0s bask amid the rippled sunlight.

The up "Royal Scot" waits to leave Glasgow Central for London Euston behind Camden Pacific 46240 "City of Coventry".

Arthur Mace travelled by overnight train from Rugby with a view to photographing the up "Royal Scot" breasting Beattock summit. He got out at Carstairs and made this picture before 7am of a 2-6-4T moving off to pick up the stock for the 7.09 train to Edinburgh.

Bletchley shed yard during the 1930's with London & North Western 2-4-2Ts and 0-8-0s.

Rugby was one of Britain's finest rail centres with five routes radiating from it. This scene at the north end of the station shows four of the famous Black 5 4-6-0s.

A rebuilt Patriot heads northwards from Rugby. These engines were ubiquitous on the southern reaches of the West Coast Main Line during the 1950s.

An L.M.S. Jubilee 4-6-0 heads south from Rugby with the Daventry radio masts in the background.

The Jubilees are popularly regarded as one of the most handsome locomotives of all times. This view of No. 45712 "Victory" at speed catches something of their magic.

The musical three cylinder throb of a Jubilee was a joy to hear and when the engines superb contours were seen amid glorious countryside the experience was complete.

The London & North Western 0-8-0s became a familiar sight on heavy shunting amongst the marshalling yards of their former empire.

An L.M.S. Stanier Black 5 4-6-0 enters Chester. The Great Western shed can be seen alongside.

The glorious days of holiday specials, once so numerous, are vividly recalled in this early 1950s scene.

London & North Western George V Class 4-4-0 "Snipe" at Chester.

Midland & Great Northern Railway 4-4-0 No.48 at Melton Constable.

Arthur Mace arranged for the Rugby School Railway Society to visit Leamington and the immaculately attired party are seen on the platform.

The Highland Railway Clan Class 4-6-0s were another classic type ousted by the Black 5s. "Clan Mackinnon" was the last survivor of these noted express engines which became extinct in 1950.

In 1950 Crewe Works had eight of Webb's 17" Coal Engines in Departmental Service around the works. All had vanished by 1953.

Midland Railway 4F 0-6-0s continued to be built by the L.M.S. until 1940. Some in the rival territory of Crewe as this late 1930s scene testifies.

Bow Works on the North London Railway with a London Tilbury & Southend 4-4-2T , a North London 0-6-0T and a Midland 3F in the background.

Breaking up London & North Western 0-8-0s in the cutting up shed at Crewe Works.

The North London Railway's solitary Crane Tank at Bow Works. Built in 1858 by Sharp Stewart - and converted to a crane engine in 1872 - this was the oldest engine to enter British Railways stock surviving until 1951.

The Lancashire and Yorkshire Railway Dreadnought 4-6-0s worked the upper reaches of the West Coast Main Line during their final years.

The Princess Royal Pacifics were the pride of the West Coast Main Line during the early 1930s. Here No. 6206 "Princess Marie Louise" stands new at Crewe curiously attached to a G.W. coach.

Bearing the London & North Western Code 1, No. 6200 "The Princess Royal" stands, a new engine in Euston Station. Notice the small Fowler tender in contrast with her later sister above.

The all enveloping atmosphere of Rugby in the 1950's is caught here as Scot Class 4-6-0, 46161 "King's Own" arrives with a Euston bound train.

L.M.S. Jubilee Class 4-6-0, 45740 "Munster" arrives at London Euston with a packed train.

L.M.S. Jubilee 45589 "Baroda" - a Leeds Holbeck engine - at Derby with the Devonian Express.

Princess Coronation Pacific 46243 "City of Lancaster". This was the only member of its class to receive a B.R. number in streamline form.

There was always a magnificent line up of engines outside Derby Works and in this view Johnson Belpaire 3P 4-4-0 and 4F 0-6-0s are seen in company with an outside framed tender from a Kirtley Goods.

The last London & North Western Railway 18" Cauliflowers hid themselves away in remote corners of the network. Note the water tank on a London & North Western tender underframe at this unknown location.

Crewe Works was the last haven for Webb's 17" 0-6-0 Coal Engines until 1953. Five hundred of these stalwarts were built between 1873 and 1892.

These pretty 2-4-2Ts were introduced by Webb during the 1890s for branch and cross country passenger work across the London & North Western system. Nicknamed "Gobblers" the last was withdrawn in 1955.

A resplendent ex-works London and North Western 0-8-0 banks an empty "loco coal" train at an unknown location.

Midland Railway 3F 0-6-0 No. 3327. Note the fine splitting distant signal in the background.

The Ben Class 4-4-0s were amongst the most elegant of Highland Railway locomotives.

Euston in the mid 1920s with London & North Western Experiment Class 4-6-0 5656 "Shark". The engine is bearing a smokebox number plate which was unusual for L.N.W. designs; she has an L.M.S. crest on the cab side and was possibly in red livery.

This up express has arrived at Euston behind two un-rebuilt Claughtons. The date is around 1927.

A London and North Western Precursor 4-4-0 arrives at Euston with an outer suburban service possibly from Bletchley or Rugby.

The Rugby to Leamington Push and Pull service stands in the Bay platform at Rugby behind a London & North Western 2-4-2T "Gobbler". The fireman has left the cramped footplate for the comfort of an adjacent trolley.

A historic moment at Crewe Works as the frames are laid for the first of Stanier's Princess Coronation Class Pacifics in 1938.

In absolute contrast, the same visit to Crewe works produced this Ramsbottom 0-6-0 Special Tank confined to works pilot duties at Wolverton. These engines were latterly overhauled at Rugby Works.

London & North Western Bissel Truck 0-4-2PT, 47865 was a rare survivor on departmental duties at Crewe Works until 1953.

This historic picture at Crewe Works shows an amazing contrast in L.M.S. freight designs with a 2-6-6-2 Garratt and a Fowler 0-8-0 in the background. The two types were built almost simultaneously during the late 20s/early 30s.

One of the lovely Highland Railway Clan Goods 4-6-0s at Inverness. In the background is a Stanier Black 5 the engines which led to the rapid demise of pre-grouping designs in the Highlands.

This picture is typical of the way in which Arthur Mace valued the fleeting instant. The scene depicts a re-built Scot entering Rugby in appalling weather.

Arthur Mace called this picture "A Crimson Rambler on its native heath." It was taken on a sunny July day in 1928 at 11.00am. The Prince of Wales in the background was heading an express from Nottingham to Llandudno.

A London and North Western 0-8-0 'Weaser' in full cry.

Jubilee Class 45591 "Udaipur" was traditionally a Crewe North engine and always a west coast one.

The un-rebuilt Patriots, descended as they were from the London & North Western Claughtons, were always thrilling to see but slightly less so if un-named like 45547 seen in typical guise at the head of a van train.

Stanier Jubilee 45712 "Victory" on an un-identified working.

On this occasion Arthur Mace was a member of a railway photographic party. The location is uncertain but is possibly the North Wales Main Line. A London and North Western Prince of Wales passes.

The opportunistic Arthur Mace often took pictures from moving trains when he saw something interesting and here he caught a London and North Western 0-8-0 piloting a war time Austerity 2-8-0.

A Webb 17" Coal Engine heads a local freight past Rugby North End.

A Midland Railway Kirtley 2-4-0 near Butterley in 1930. These engines ended their life on the Kettering to Cambridge line.

A superb study of London & North Western Coal Tank No.7802 at Llandudno in L.M.S. days.

When travelling north up the West Coast Main Line the first Caledonian engines would be encountered at Carlisle working from Kingmoor Depot. This 0-6-0T is seen on station pilot duties at Carlisle Citadel Station.

An unidentified London & North Western engine enters Rugby in this highly atmospheric scene complete with period train spotters. The girder bridge carrying the Great Central Main Line over the West Coast Main Line heightens the mood.

Derby Shed yard in 1929 with Belpaire and 2P 4-4-0s, new Fowler 2-6-4T No. 2360 and tenders from Royal Scot 4-6-0s of which number 6150 to 6169 were built there the following year.

The beautiful lines of the Caledonian Railway 4-6-0s was continued in these Pickersgill engines of 1916. All had vanished by 1953.

Arthur Mace was on a party visit to Crewe works in the summer of 1939 when the decimation of London & North Western types was well under way. Visible here are Precursors, Prince of Wales, Coal Tanks, Bissel Truck, Panniers and George Vs.

Fowler 2-6-4T No. 42319, one of 125 engines built for the L.M.S. between 1927 and 1934.

A Caledonian Railway 0-4-4T at Edinburgh Princes Street Station albeit that she is bearing a 27C Hamilton shedplate.

The centenary of the London and Birmingham Railway was held at Euston in 1938 and amongst the exhibits were the Liverpool and Manchester Railway's "Lion" and a streamlined Duchess. The Coronation Scot train is in the background.

Also present were London & North Western single Cornwall and George V 4-4-0 No. 25348 "Coronation" - the 5,000th engine built at Crewe.

The Edwardian styling of the London & North Western Precursor introduced in 1904 is apparent in this study of No. 5316 "Viscount".

The last Precursor to remain in service was No. 25297 "Sirocco". There was a preservation attempt which tragically failed, leaving a massive gap in locomotive history.

A London and North Western 4-4-0 trundles a brake van along one of the North Wales branches in 1930.

An L.M.S. Simple 2P 4-4-0 Bearing a 2E Northampton shed code.

Stanier Black 5 No. 5057 picks up water at speed. The location is possibly Dunsmore troughs between Rugby and Nuneaton.

Re-built Patriot 5536 "Private W. Wood V.C." picks up water whilst overtaking a fast freight. Notice the containers being carried in open wagons.

Arthur Mace's description of this picture of Patriot 45512 "Bunsen" reads 'The Irish Mail in a hurry.' The train is seen picking up water at Aber troughs (milepost 233) on the North Wales Main Line.

A fine period scene of Midland Railway Johnson 2-4-0 No.257 at Hitchin presumably working the Hitchin to Bedford line.

This scene of a London & North Western Jumbo 2-4-0 piloting a Prince of Wales 4-6-0 at Euston dates around the time of the grouping in 1923.

A Caledonian Railway's Dunalastair 4-4-0 designed by McIntosh in 1910.

The gaunt Edwardian form of the London & North Western Precursor decked in Blackberry black livery is shown to full effect in this superb evocation. The Precursor is fitted with an original round top boiler.

A Black 5 4-6-0 pilots an un-rebuilt Patriot. Notice that the water troughs are set only on the fast lines.

Many Black 5s were sent to Scotland to replace a multitude of ageing pre-grouping designs. This one is at work in the Highlands. Note the snow fence wires in the background.

An L.M.S. Black 5, 4-6-0 fitted for test running at Rugby shed. The girder bridge carrying the Great Central Main Line is in the background.

The short lived Kentish Belle - later known as the Thanet Belle - behind King Arthur Class 4-6-0 No. 30763 "Sir Bors de Ganis".

Folkestone Central Station bridge.

Schools Class 30920 "Rugby" couples on to a boat train at Folkestone Junction.

The glorious N15X Class 4-6-0 "Remembrance" at Nine Elms. These engines were re-built from Brighton Baltic 4-6-4Ts.

Schools Class No. 30909 "St Paul's" heading special narrow bodied stock for the Hastings line.

King Arthur No. 30768 "Sir Balin" was the pride of Stewarts Lane. She is seen here on a Ramsgate train.

King Arthur Class 4-6-0 No. 30781 "Sir Aglovale" with an Ocean Liner express boat train from Victoria to Dover.

King Arthur Class 4-6-0 No. 30792 "Sir Hervis de Revel" at Broadstairs with a Pick- up Goods.

A Tonbridge to Brighton train headed by L Class 31771 crosses the London Road viaduct at Brighton.

One of the Newhaven Harbour Company's Terriers at Sheffield Park. She was formerly London Brighton & South Coast No. 72 "Fenchurch".

A South Eastern and Chatham Railway B1 Class 4-4-0

A South Eastern and Chatham Railway H Class 0-4-4-T with an SEC coach and two LBSC coaches.

A London & South Western Railway Push-Pull fitted M7 0-4-4T at Horsham.

An L Class 4-4-0 passes Hither Green with a Down Folkestone.

A London Brighton and South Coast B4X 4-4-0 with the down 5.05 London Bridge to Eastbourne at Forest Hill. The clerestory coach was once part of the L.B.S.C.'s royal train.

A D1 Class 4-4-0 with a lattice post London Chatham and Dover Railway signal.

Britannia Pacific No. 70014 "Iron Duke" with the Golden Arrow. Following their introduction in 1951, these engines replaced Bulleid's Pacifics on this working.

The Devon Belle, one of Britain's most glorious trains at Exeter Central behind Merchant Navy Class No. 35007 "Aberdeen Commonwealth".

"The Man of Kent " behind Bulleid West Country Pacific No. 34097 "Holsworthy".

"The Man of Kent" at Folkestone Central behind Bulleid Battle of Britain Pacific No. 34082 "615 Squadron".

An H Class 0-4-4T at Minster Junction on the South Eastern Railway route to Ramsgate.

A re-built South Eastern & Chatham Railway Stirling Class F1 4-4-0 in a superb composition in which the railway is the stage and the train the actor.

A London & South Western Railway Adams O2 Class 0-4-4T emerges from the tunnel at Ventnor on the Isle of Wight.

London & South Western Railway T9 Class "Greyhound" 4-4-0 No. 288 with Great Western clerestory coaches during the early 1920s - possibly on a Birkenhead to Bournemouth working.

South Eastern & Chatham H Class No. 31544 on a Tunbridge Wells to Oxted push and pull train.

A Southern Railway L Class 4-4-0 at the head of a Folkestone train.

South Eastern & Chatham Class D1 4-4-0 No. 31749 heads an up train at Sittingbourne Junction (for Sheerness).

Southern Railway N Class 2-6-0 No. 1407 built at Ashford Works in 1933.

A South Eastern & Chatham Stirling O Class relegated to stationary boiler service at Ramsgate for carriage heating. The Ramsgate breakdown crane is in the background.

A South Eastern & Chatham R1 Class 0-4-4T possibly on a Westerham Branch train.

South Eastern & Chatham C Class No. 31243 shunting at Dover docks.

A South Eastern and Chatham O1 Class re-built Stirling 0-6-0 of 1878 with outside framed tender. These engines were blessed with great longevity the last examples surviving until 1961.

Canterbury West signal box with Classes H 0-4-4T and N 2-6-0 visible. The old Canterbury and Whitstable Railway engine shed can be seen in the background.

This amazing scene represents Arthur Mace at his best. The location is Folkestone harbour and the engine one of Stirling's Class R Domeless 0-6-0Ts. The picture is a masterpiece by any standards but the nun elevates the scene to a sublime dimension.

A Southern Railway N Class 2-6-0 crosses the street at Canterbury. The period A.A. motor cycle and pram evoke the Picture Post element in Arthur Mace's work.

A Southern Railway "Mechanical Horse" which replaced the traditional railway horse drawn delivery drays.

Southern Railway L Class 4-4-0 No. 31781 the last of its class to be built,crosses the main road at Canterbury.

A South Eastern & Chatham H Class 0-4-4T completes this Picture Post styled trilogy at Canterbury.

A South Eastern & Chatham Railway Class B1 4-4-0.

A Southern Railway L Class 4-4-0 leaves Ramsgate.

Brighton Atlantic 2424 "Beachy Head" on Ramsgate shed! Following the mid-Sussex electrification, some of these engines worked from Stewarts Lane on Ramsgate services during the summer of 1938. A London Chatham & Dover Railway bogie coach is in the background.

One of the L.M.S. Ivatt 2-6-2Ts allocated to the Southern Region during the 1950s.

A Southern Railway U1 Class 2-6-0 at East Grinstead Low Level with a Victoria to Brighton train via Sheffield Park.

South Eastern & Chatham Railway D1 Class 4-4-0 No. 31145 at an unknown location with a Dover boat train approaching

One of Marsh's unsuccessful London Brighton & South Coast I1 Class 4-4-2Ts at East Croydon during the early 1920s. These engines were later re-built by Maunsell to become Class I1X. Note the overhead electrification.

London Brighton & South Coast Class E2 0-6-0T No. 103 shunting at Forest Hill.

Arthur Mace often made sets of pictures at a given location. Three successive trains pass during the same lineside stint. His ragged inclusion of the "No Trespassing" board is clearly not an accident and may have been a wry aside to the fact that he was so close to the running line. The picture (top) shows an L.B.&S.C. C2X Class 0-6-0 the lower left is an L.B.&S.C. Stroudly B1 0-4-2 and lower right an L.B.&S.C. E4 0-6-2T.

A touch of Arthur Mace's sense of the ridiculous is indicated in this unique study of the afternoon miner's special approaching the Chislet Colliery Halt on the Kent coalfield behind an L.M.S. designed Fairburn 2-6-4T.

A South Eastern & Chatham H Class 0-4-4T at Minster.

A party visit to Hither Green Shed with cameras focused on an N Class 2-6-0 as a C Class 0-6-0 simmers alongside.

Two of R.J. Billington's characteristic LBSC Radial Tanks double-heading back to back a train of antique wooden-bodied coaches.

Tunbridge Wells West with (left) an H Class 0-4-4T from Oxted, D1 Class 4-4-0 No. 31470 approaching with a Tonbridge to Brighton train and an L Class 4-4-0 in the Bay platform.

A Bricklayers Arms based Southern Railway N Class 2-6-0 heads a freight along the South Eastern main line.

Southern Railway King Arthur Class 4-6-0 30765 "Sir Gareth" at Broadstairs with a superb rake of new Mark 1 coaches.

Southern Railway Schools Class 4-4-0 No. 30917 "Ardingly" with a Kent Coast Line train which includes one Pullman in the rake.

Bulleid Battle of Britain Pacific No.34082 "615 Squadron" arriving at Folkestone Priory with a down train.

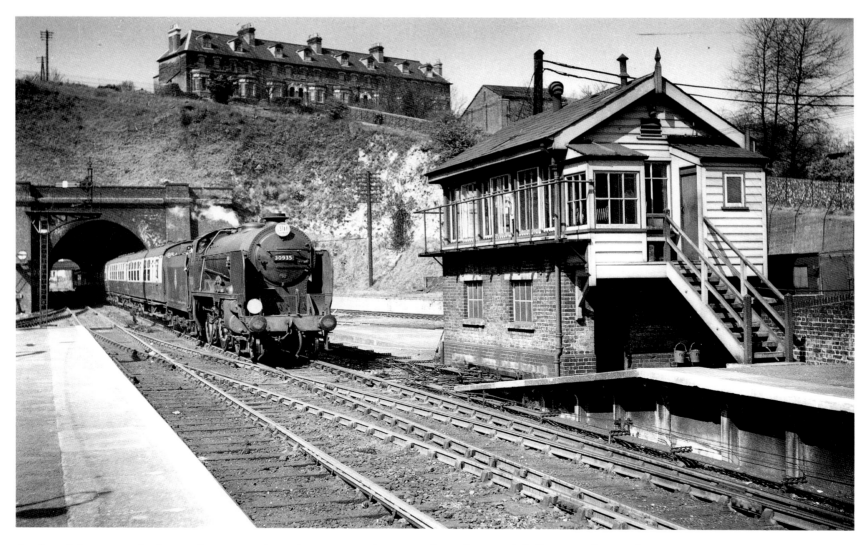

Arthur Mace regularly made successive pictures on the same location and following from above is Schools Class 4-4-0 No. 30935 "Sevenoaks".

A Southern Region U1 Class 2-6-0 at the eastern side of Victoria Station with a relief Ramsgate express.

Chivalry in the rain as a D1 Class 4-4-0 prepares for departure on the Kent Coast Line.

The Great North of Scotland Railway's D41 4-4-0s with 6'1"diameter driving wheels were one of the most elegant designs to grace British metals. Introduced in 1893 they consisted of a class of 32 engines and appeared on both passenger and mixed freight workings.

Two Southern Railway Schools Class 4-4-0s at Waterloo both on Portsmouth trains.

This King Arthur is one of the batch numbered between 793 and 806 which were distinctive in having six wheeled tenders for working the Brighton line.

Southern Railway Schools Class 4-4-0 No. 30938 "St. Olave's" with Mark 1 coaches in tow.

A King Arthur heads a pick-up freight near Broadstairs. It is a sober thought that the very concept of such a train today would be beyond our wildest imagination!

A heavy coal train trundles along the Great Central Main Line behind re-built O1 Class 2-8-0 No. 63806.

An original Great Eastern Class B12 4-6-0 complete with ACFI feed water heater approaches Sheringham with a Midland & Great Northern Line train.

A1 Pacific No. 60124 "Kenilworth" passes Peterborough Crescent Junction on the East Coast Main Line.

During the early 1950s, a batch of A3 Pacifics - including "Flying Scotsman" - were drafted on to the Great Central Main Line for working between London Marylebone and Manchester. Also in the batch was No. 60052 "Prince Palatine" seen here after its return to the Great Northern Main Line as a Leeds Copley Hill engine.

North British D30 Scott Class 4-4-0 62423 "Dugald Dalgetty" bearing a Hawick shedplate.

This scene is dated 1946/7 the time of the L.N.E.R. re-numbering. The Gresley V2 2-6-2 has drawn well up in the platform of this unknown location and threatens to obscure the view of the A4 Pacific approaching at speed much to the chagrin of the train spotters who are in a clear state of emotional agitation.

North Eastern Railway Class B13 4-6-0 No. 1699 at Rugby where it acted as a counter pressure engine at the test plant. The foreigner is even bearing an improvised 2A shedplate.

One of Ivatt's large boilered C1 Class Atlantics of the Great Northern Railway.

A Great Northern K2 " Ragtimer " 2-6-0 on the Great Eastern section at Norwich Station.

An L.N.E.R. Scottish Director 4-4-0 at Princes Street Gardens Edinburgh.

North British Glen Class No. 62426 "Cuddie Headrigg", a Perth engine, heads a local train.

From 1925, the L.N.E.R. ordered 50 of these Sentinel Steam Railcars for branch line services. Others were built by the Clayton Wagon Works in Lincoln. They were named after famous stagecoaches of the past like Chevy Chase, Bang Up and Rapid. This example, seen hauling a van, anticipates the diesel multiple unit of thirty years later.

The London & North Western also had some steam rail motors for branch line work which they built at Crewe. The only comment Arthur Mace made about the picture was "The last of the Clan". Date and location un-identified.

Two classic Great Central designs at Liverpool Brunswick Shed . On the left under repair is Class D10 Director 4-4-0 62658 "Prince George" with Class J11 Pom Pom 0-6-0 No. 64304.

Gresley Class A3 Pacific No. 60097 "Humorist" decked with A1 type windshields attracts the keen attention of the train spotter. This engine was the guinea pig of the A3s being subjected to a number of experimental modifications.

The majesty of the L.N.E.R. A4s is summed up in this scene of No. 60011 "Empire of India" having arrived at Kings Cross with The Elizabethan from Edinburgh.

L.N.E.R. A4 Pacific No. 60034 "Lord Farringdon" during the famous locomotive exchanges of 1948. The location is unknown but she is clearly off her home territory judging by the intense interest being shown by the crowd of on-lookers.

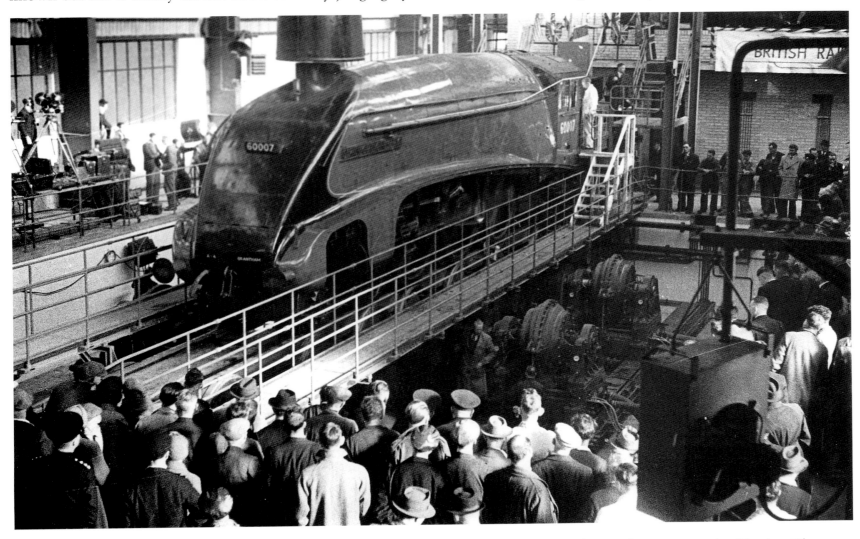

Sister engine No. 60007 "Sir Nigel Gresley" is seen being put through its paces at the Rugby Locomotive Testing Plant.

Verney Junction on the Metropolitan & Great Central Joint with an ex-Manchester Sheffield & Lincolnshire Railway Class F1 2-4-2T introduced in 1889.

A North Eastern Railway Class J71 0-6-0T at Alne on the Easingwold Railway.

Manchester Sheffield & Lincolnshire Railway N5 Class 0-6-2T No. 69293. The type was introduced in 1891 and an engine of this class had the distinction of being the first British locomotive to be fitted with a Belpaire Firebox.

A Great Northern Ivatt N1 0-6-2T fitted with condensing pipes. She is seen at Hither Green during the early 1920s having worked a transfer freight from Hornsey.

A South Eastern & Chatham E Class 4-4-0. The location is unknown - possibly Faversham? Engine Duty No. 94 was a Bricklayers Arms diagram. A D1 4-4-0 adds or detaches a vehicle in the background.

Robinson's Great Central Railway 2-8-0s introduced in 1911 were one of Britain's premier freight designs. Many were built for the Railway Operating Division during World War One and subsequently worked abroad during the war effort. Apart from prolific work in Britain the type also saw service overseas during World War Two.

A Great Central Director 4-4-0 at Liverpool Brunswick Depot for working on the Cheshire Lines Committee network.

Robinson's passenger designs for the Great Central were little short of works of art. Many classes were introduced including the famous Fish Engines for working express fish trains to London at passenger train speeds. No. 5195 is a B1 Class 4-6-0 introduced in 1903 and one of only two built.

A fine diversity of interest at an unknown location. On the left is a Great Northern Ivatt J3 Class 0-6-0 the last example of which was withdrawn in 1953. Alongside stands a Class N5 Manchester Sheffield & Lincolnshire Pollitt 0-6-2T with a Great Western Iron Mink wagon.

A North British Railway Class J36 0-6-0 on branch line duties in Scotland.

The atmosphere of a country branch line is epitomised in this scene at the end of the line on the Easingwold Railway with a North Eastern Class J71 0-6-0T.

One of Johnson's original Midland Railway 4-4-0s classified C by the Midland & Great Northern Joint Railway, leaves Sheringham for King's Lynn during the 1930s.

No. 67460 was one of two North British Class C15 4-4-2Ts to be motor fitted for branch line work between Craigendoran Junction and Arrochar along the bank of Loch Lomond and through Glen Douglas. Allocated to Glasgow Eastfield they outlived other members of the class until replaced by diesel railcars in 1959.

"The Master Cutler" arrives at London Marylebone behind Gresley A3 Pacific No.60102 "Sir Fredrick Banbury".

A Great Northern line up at Nottingham Victoria with a K2 "Ragtimer" 2-6-0 on the left with a pair of Ivatt J6 0-6-0s.

One of the numerous War Department Austerity 2-8-0s of which 733 were built for operations during World War Two. After the hostilities they were put to work in many parts of Britain. They were regarded as mongrels devoid of any lineage. Invariably grubby and rough to ride they were good hauling engines and some lasted almost until the end of steam.

Durham Station in more exciting times with a Gresley Class V2 2-6-2 on the left and an A3 Pacific.

A large boilered Great Northern Atlantic at speed.

L.N.E.R. Shire Class D49 No.62708 "Argyllshire".

Large boilered Ivatt Great Northern C1 Class Atlantic No.3276 heads a Sheffield to Swindon express comprised of G.W.R. stock.

The tender of a BR Standard Class 76000 during building at The Plant in Doncaster.

Doncaster Works had the delightful habit of applying this snowflake effect to engines in the paintshop prior to final finishing. Awaiting restoration to full glory is A1 Class 4-6-2 Pacific No. 60136 "Alcazar".

In 1951 the newly formed British Railways selected upon twelve standard designs to replace the wide diversity of types inherited from the previous companies. The Standards were all built in the traditional railway works of the big four companies and these scenes show the Class 3 76000 2-6-0s under construction at Doncaster Works in the mid 1950s.

Scottish Director 4-4-0 No. 62673 "Evan Dhu". These engines are descended directly from Robinson's Directors for the Great Central Railway and were built in 1924 for service in Scotland.

A Colwick allocated Great Northern K2 2-6-0 possibly on a Nottingham to Grantham train.

Scottish Director 4-4-0 No. 62691 "Laird of Balmawhapple" emerges from Princes Street tunnel Edinburgh.

The Midland & Great Northern Joint Railway's No. 86 was originally a Great Northern Ivatt DA Class 0-6-0. She was not built at Doncaster but by Dubs in Polmadie Glasgow as the diamond shaped worksplate reveals.

A stranger at Norwich Station in the form of a North Eastern Railway Class J21 0-6-0. The anomaly is the result of an exchange whereby some Great Eastern E4 2-4-0s had been transferred to work the Bishops Castle line and the J21s were given in exchange. This arrangement lasted from 1935 to 1942.

North British Class J35 0-6-0 No.64484 emerges from Princes Street Gardens north of Edinburgh Waverley.

The Midland & Great Northern Joint Railway's No. 88 was also a Great Northern Ivatt DA Class 0-6-0 built by Dubs. These engines, in common with all the M. & G.N.'s roster were maintained in the company's works in the small Norfolk town of Melton Constable. This works also built a number of indigenous engines.

The shape which inspired the nation. Nigel Gresley's A3 Pacifics for the L.N.E.R. caught the public's imagination both with their striking appearance and unprecedented high speed running. The example shown here is Edinburgh Haymarket's "Brown Jack"

One of Edward Thomson's L.N.E.R. Class L1 2-6-2T on a running in turn, brand new.

West Runton Station board on the Midland & Great Northern Joint Railway.

An L.N.E.R. V1 Class 2-6-2 emerges from Princes Street Gardens Edinburgh.

These pictures belong to a whole series Arthur Mace made of various trains emerging from these tunnels.

Double heading with heavy holiday trains over the Midland & Great Northern Joint Railway was not uncommon and here No. 39, a re-boilered Midland Railway Johnson 4-4-0 pilots a Beyer Peacock built 4-4-0.

Midland & Great Northern Joint Railway Beyer Peacock 4-4-0 No. 30 approaches Sheringham.

Holden Great Eastern Class D15 4-4-0 No.8883.

The 4-4-0s on the Midland & Great Northern Joint performed prestigious feats of haulage with heavy holiday trains. Here No. 44, a Class C re-boilered Midland 4-4-0 approaches Melton Constable from Yarmouth.

Great Western 2-6-2T No.4167 at Birmingham Snow Hill Station.

The up Mayflower express Plymouth to Paddington arrives at Exeter behind a King Class 4-6-0.

The Bristolian, having arrived at Paddington.

An up train at Birmingham Snow Hill headed by Great Western Castle Class No. 5063 "Earl Baldwin".

This line-up of celebrity types at Swindon Works embraces three generations of Great Western 4-6-0s. From the left Castle Class 5039 "Rhuddlan Castle"; Star Class 4007 "Swallowfield Park" and King Class No. 6020 "King Henry IV".

A Great Western 4-4-0 - presumably a Bulldog - in the cutting up shop at Swindon Works.

Great Western King Class 4-6-0 No.6028 "King George VI" undergoes overhaul at Swindon works.

Swindon locomotive works A Shop.

One of the Cambrian Railway's delightful Edwardian 0-6-0s.

One hundred of Robinson's Great Central 2-8-0s were purchased by the Great Western from the War Department following the first world war. This example was caught sporting a Great Western Class 47XX chimney.

Swindon, along with Derby, Doncaster and Crewe was one of the railway towns. It represented British industry at its peak. This scene in Swindon A Shop testifies to halcyon days past in a town whose railway traditions have been decimated.

Swindon running shed had a large and diverse allocation and this study in the Roundhouse includes one of the twenty Dean Goods 0-6-0s which had outside frames.

The down Cornishman at Bristol Temple Meads.

Great Western King Class 4-6-0 No.6005 "King George II".

A Star at Oxford. Great Western 4-6-0 No.4049 "Princess Maud" with the London & North Western engine shed in the background.

Another of Arthur Mace's opportunistic pictures taken in the instant on Reading Station. A father holds up his child to watch the majestic passage of Castle Class 4-6-0 No.7011 "Banbury Castle" approaching on the fast line.

Great Western Hall Class 4-6-0 No.5920 "Wycliffe Hall" in company with London & North Western signals.

A pair of Great Western Castle Class 4-6-0s at Bristol Temple Meads Station. On the left is No.5089 "Westminster Abbey" with No.5050 "Earl of St. Germans".

"Skylark" was one of the last two surviving Great Western Bulldog 4-4-0s - the other being "Seagull". Both were allocated to Reading and had gone by 1951.

A Great Western 1400 Class 0-4-2T at Moretonhampstead.

Great Western Hawkesworth 0-6-0PT No.9475 at Leamington.

Great Western 5700 Class 0-6-0PT No.9654 caught at Witney on the Fairford Branch from Oxford.

A blue liveried Great Western King Class 4-6-0 leaving Exeter.

Great Western County Class 4-6-0 No.1006 "County of Cornwall" at Penzance.

Great Western 5700 Class 0-6-0PT No.9654 at Fairford.

A down stopper at Truro headed by Great Western Grange Class 4-6-0 No.6871 "Bourton Grange". Notice how full the sidings are complete with obligatory shunter. Included in the rakes is a gas tank wagon for refuelling restaurant cars.

A Great Western County Class 4-6-0 on the up Cornishman near Penzance.

This Castle is in light green experimental livery. She is No.4089 "Donnington Castle" and is seen at Penzance.

Great Western Hall Class No.6992 "Arborfield Hall" enters Hereford from the south.

A County Class 4-6-0 passes Newbury. In the background is a Great Western Diesel Railcar working the Lambourn branch and in the far distance what appears to be a Midland & South Western Junction Railway 2-4-0.

Great Western 2800 Class 2-8-0 No.3842 heading a freight train at an unknown location.

A mixed train at Swindon Junction with Great Western 2-4-0 Metro Tank No.1486 trailing a gas tank wagon for refuelling restaurant cars, a milk van and a horse box.

Midland & South Western Junction Railway 2-4-0 No.1335 heads a down freight through Newbury. These lovely engines were built in 1894 and by the time the last one disappeared in 1954, the 2-4-0 tender engine had become little more than a memory.

These Monks Ferry locomotive coal wagons have wooden bodies and consist of three containers in an underframe.

The excitement of a busy Great Western main line station is conjured up by this scene. On the left is Castle Class No.5031 "Totnes Castle" alongside Star Class No.4026. This engine was named "Japanese Monarch" but after the outbreak of World War Two its name evoked distaste and the plates were removed. The engine ran nameless for the remainder of it's life.

County Class 4-6-0 No.1008 "County of Cardigan" passes milepost 205 on the Great Western Main Line.

A down express at Didcot headed by Castle Class 4-6-0 No.4086 "Builth Castle".

A Great Western 56XX Class 0-6-2T at Birmingham Snow Hill Station.

A brace of Great Western Collett Class 2251 0-6-0s.

A Great Western Flower Class 4-4-0 at Chester with a London & North Western coach.

Dukedog No.9012 at Machynlleth. These engines were built from withdrawn Duke of Cornwall Class boilers (see page 168/169) and withdrawn Bulldog frames (page 152/153). Following their inception in 1936 some carried the name of Earls until these were transferred to newly built Castle Class engines.

Great Western Duke Class 4-4-0 No.3252 "Duke of Cornwall" at Shrewsbury. The second coach in the formation is of Cambrian origin.

The Cornish Riviera Express at Paddington with a King Class 4-6-0.

The Cambrian Coast Express at Birmingham Snow Hill behind Great Western King Class 4-6-0 No.6026 "King John".

A down train at Reading headed by Castle Class No.5036 "Lyonshall Castle".

The hallowed portals of Old Oak Common Shed in West London are host to Castle Class 4096 "Highclere Castle".

Great Western Saint Class No.2946 "Langford Court" at Exeter St. David's

Arthur Mace has captured the full excitement of a departing express as felt by the train spotter as he watched Castle Class No.5025 "Chirk Castle" depart from Birmingham Snow Hill.

A Great Western Grange Class 4-6-0 at Penzance.

A Great Western 4500 Class 2-6-2T arrives at St. Ives having traversed the branch from St. Erth on the Great Western Main Line.

The down Pembroke Coast Express passes Didcot behind Castle Class 4-6-0 No.4089 "Donnington Castle".

Banbury Station after re-building with a King Class 4-6-0 at the head of an up Wolverhampton-Paddington express.

A Chipping Norton train at Banbury headed by Great Western 14XX Class 0-4-2T No.1401.

The Great Western made extensive use of the 0-4-2T for motor work on branch trains and these original engines all date back to the 1870s/80s. The most famous was "Fair Rosamund" the only one named and the regular engine on the Oxford to Woodstock branch for some forty years. In 1932 the 1400 Class were introduced as a modern variant. Here, one of the original engines is seen at West Kirby on the Wirral.

Great Western Barnum Class 2-4-0 No.3223 enters Crewe with a train from Wellington.

Great Western Collett Class 2251 0-6-0 No.3212 at Newbury.

The Oswestry train in the Bay at Gobowen headed by Great Western 1400 Class 0-4-2T No.1432.

Cambrian Railway 2-4-0T No.1197 at Oswestry. She was one of two engines built in 1866 and withdrawn in 1948.

A Wellington train at Crewe headed by Great Western 2-4-0T No.3201.

The Cambrian Coast Express arrives at Shrewsbury with Dukedog No.9017 piloting a Manor Class 4-6-0.

Great Southern Railway of Ireland Class D14 4-4-0 No.89 built in 1891.

Great Southern Railway of Ireland Class J15 0-6-0, a standard type introduced in 1866 as a 'Maid of All Work' and a highly successful design which survived until the mid 1960s.

Londonderry & Lough Swilly Railway 3' gauge 4-8-4T No.5 built by Hudswell Clark of Leeds in 1912. These were the largest narrow gauge locomotives in the British Isles.

Great Southern Railway of Ireland 4-6-0 No.402. This locomotive which dates back to 1921 originally had four cylinders but was later re-built as a two cylinder engine.

Great Southern Railway of Ireland 5' 3" gauge 4-6-0 No.187.

An ex-Tralee & Dingle Railway 3' gauge Class KN2 2-6-0T built by Kerr Stewart of Stoke-on-Trent. She was caught working on the C.I.E's Cavan and Leitrim section with the 1.50pm Ballinamore to Arigna branch train on the 23rd of August 1954.

Great Northern Railway of Ireland T2 Class 4-4-2T No.144 at an unknown location.

A Great Southern & Western Railway of Ireland 5' 3" gauge Class J15 0-6-0 at an unknown rural location.

Horseboxes for Bertram Mills Circus recalling those glorious pre-motorway days when railways handled the nation's transport needs in a safe, efficient and environmentally disciplined way.

Arthur Mace produced this picture during a party visit to London Transport's Lillie Bridge depot. The engines L30 and L31 are 0-6-0Ts and the only examples of their type.

Dublin Wicklow & Wexford warning sign.

No. L51 a London Transport 0-6-2T at Lillie Bridge depot.

Unidentified semaphore.

Unidentified semaphore.

A Sentinel in industrial use on the Oxfordshire ironstone system at Wroxton near Banbury.

One of the locomotives from Arthur Guinness's St. James Gate Brewery in Dublin. This was served by eight miles of 1' 10" gauge railway which included a gradient of 1 in 39.

A scene on the 2' 3" gauge Tallylyn Railway which was one of the last narrow gauge lines to remain active in Britain. Avid fund raising in 1951 saved this railway and triggered the Railway Preservation Movement.

Another study of the 1' 10" gauge locomotives which worked Arthur Guinness and Co. Ltd. Brewery in Dublin. With cylinders placed above the boiler these engines could be mounted on haulage wagons for use on the 5' 3" gauge. Most were built between 1882 and 1891 by the Cork Street Foundry Dublin.

East Kent Railway No.100 was a South Eastern & Chatham Class 01 0-6-0. She was formerly Southern Railway No.1383.

Metropolitan Railway 4-4-0T No.23 at Brill in 1935. This branch from Quainton Road was the last haunt of these superb engines which in their final days trundled its length hauling one eight wheeled Oldbury coach of 1865 vintage. The branch closed later the same year on November 30th.

Metropolitan Railway 4-4-0T No.41 at Quainton Road.

Great Southern Railway of Ireland 4-4-0 No.11 on the scrap line at Inchicore Works. Classified D17, these engines were introduced in 1883. By the time of their withdrawal they had acquired a superb vintage aura accentuated by their low slung boilers, tall chimneys 6' 7" diameter driving wheels, high splashers and centrally opening smokebox doors and outside framed tender.

This was one of Arthur Mace's first railway pictures and one of his best. The date is possibly 1921 when he was 13 years old. It was taken somewhere in the South London area and the fine lady using her umbrella as a parasol is probably his mother. The passing train is headed by a London Brighton & South Coast B4 Class 4-4-0. This print has been reproduced in its present condition, un-touched as a period piece of classic railway photography from three-quarters of a century ago.